T0083801

# THE THIRTEENTH MONTH

# *The Thirteenth Month*

INGE PEDERSEN

Translated from the Danish by Marilyn Nelson

FIELD Translation Series 27
Oberlin College Press

http://www.oberlin.edu/ocpress

The FIELD Translation Series, Volume 27

Pedersen, Inge.
       *The Thirteenth Month* / Inge Pedersen; translated by
       Marilyn Nelson.
       (The FIELD Translation Series) v.27
       I. Title.   II. Series.

LC:  2005933385
ISBN-13:  978-0-932440-36-5
ISBN-10:  0-932440-36-3

# ACKNOWLEDGMENTS

The author would like to thank the Danish Arts Agency, *Kunststyrelsen*, and the Danish Arts Foundation, *Statens Kunstfond*, for their support of this publication.

The translator would like to thank the Heinrich Böll Foundation for the two-week residency in Böll's cottage on Achill Island, Ireland, during which she and the author began this work.

Both give grateful acknowledgment to the original publishers of some of these translations: *Arts and Letters* ("A Stone in the Belly," "The Thirteenth Month," "Vertical"), *Blackbird* ("Thank-You Note," "Wound," "Circle," "The Potatoes"), *Connecticut River Review* ("Tight-Rope Dancer," "Room Service"), *FIELD* ("Blue," "Wild Pursuit," "Salt," "Weasel," "Open the Darkness," "The Move"), *Frigate* ("A Shared Second" [as "As If in the Dark"], "Towards Morning"), *The Journal* ("When I'm Eaten by Ants," "Right There in the Smoke"), and *The Massachusetts Review* ("Chimneysweep").

# CONTENTS

# TRANSLATOR'S INTRODUCTION

Inge Pedersen and I first met as neighbors and colleagues some thirty years ago when I spent a year teaching at Nørre Nissum Seminarium, a small college of education in a village near the west coast of Jutland, in Denmark. Inge and her husband, Bent, and their three charming children became my instant good friends, she and I discovering in each other an immediate affinity which came to full bloom only years later, after the trauma of tragically losing one of her sons had driven Inge to poetry.

In summer 2000 I visited Inge in Denmark. Her first copies of her new book arrived at her house on the day I arrived. A few glasses of champagne later, I had offered to translate it. I put my hand to it as soon as I got back to the States, with the growing and humbling realization that both my Danish and my two-volume Danish/English dictionary were woefully inadequate. But in 2001 I won a two-week residency at the simple cottage once owned by Nobel Prize-winning German novelist Heinrich Böll on Achill Island in Ireland, and I invited Inge to join me. There we sat every morning in Böll's workspace, a light, cool, sparsely furnished room, discussing our poems and our thoughts about translation. I came home with notes which, aided by several e-mail exchanges, became finished translations of 19 of Inge's poems. We completed the manuscript during the fall of 2004, when she and her husband spent two weeks at my home in Connecticut.

Two of the poems in this collection are published here for the first time. Others are taken from Inge's collections *Leve med Kulden* (1982), *Sejlads paa en Ø* (1985), *Simultan* (1988), *Den Trettende Maaned* (2000), and *Et Lille Stykke Luft* (2003).

*Marilyn Nelson*

# THE THIRTEENTH MONTH

# TOWARDS MORNING

Towards morning
I ride high in the saddle:
scram
or you're dead meat
I snarl at all
the small rodents in my heart

the day is a falcon
on my shoulder

# WEASEL

Then as now, the same whetted
light of March,
I can hear it hone
itself blue on the snow. With the sled's
lurching chop against my ankles
the only thought in my head is home. And then scram,
get lost, you snotty little worms! The big
boys' adolescent voices break
and echo, grinning like the weasel they say
hides in the sledding hill. Its gleaming gape
of bluish teeth could crush my heels
so they shatter like glass.
And like bones, like naked cartilage, then
as now, the snow is blue.
I hear March gnawing.

# RESPITE

The sky and the trees
begin on the wall
paper to wake as light
and shadows
vibrating forest
that sings under the roof
under the pillow and close
to my ear
a blackbird's throat

and the clouds fly
in the mirror
because no one I love
died last night
nor was anyone found last night
white and outstretched
in their beds

and across the floor
out through the window
streams the grass
cool
still a bit wet
down through a fragrant
hazy meadow
I hop and jump
and forget

forget in the grass
and the blackbird's sound

# CHIMNEYSWEEP

Only in a glimpse can I remember the wind
that snatched at a young chimneysweep's
trousers one flapping
winter morning, as he climbed up
out of a trapdoor onto a roof. And in a glimpse the snow
and believe it or not
the sun was red
as he took a deep drag off an old butt. Maybe
his bearded cheeks sucked in
with the fandango he jumped up to dance
on the edge of a chimney, with the towers and turrets
lying under his feet. And the cars deep
in the bottom of the street I remember only
as black harem-girls with downcast eyes
dressed in slowly descending feathers. Perhaps
he fell. But that it is possible
to own everything appeared to me with brilliant clarity
as the sun rose.

# MY GRANDMOTHER SITS IN THE GARDEN

She was
blue blue eyes
smile and wrinkles
winter apple
once
a patient angel
who played cards with me
for hours at a time
a little bitty shape
in a white bed
the blue oxygen bottles
had come to take her away
and then she was gone

she became a photograph over my desk
an old woman
in the shadow of a bush neglected and
ordinary in her garden
became a picture of hands
over a checkered apron
over a fat belly
when she chatted with me
I saw a photograph

but now I walk in the dark with bare feet
in the rain-cooled grass
with every step
closer:
she who is allowed to have a fat belly
because fourteen children lived there

it is their beautiful house
closer:
her face
which kept itself alive
closer:
a cloud of flowers
a rare, fragrant bush
with a dream name
closer:
now my grandmother is sitting in the garden

# CIRCLE

    Want
an evening with dark
blue frostcrust shining
on the snow around the house
and my knees
in the hollow of yours
my nose against your back
my hand on your warm
sleeping belly
    Want
an evening with hot
blue asphalt
and sweet wickedness
my gaze
on the curve
of another man's back
till I am an animal panting
to surrender to
    Want
everything that I
don't
    Want

# THE FIRST SPRING'S SHADOW

A steep, muddy path past a field with cows and down through the woods, where you might expect to come upon a forest lake. A sun that pling, pling leaps out between the dark tree trunks and hits the chrome of the bicycles, as they ride ever faster and steeper downhill. The moist new leaves of beeches swipe against her face, and at the sight of his back, all its devil-may-care energy, a smile bubbles up in the corners of her mouth and makes the woods so dense that you might imagine a bellowing stag would soon appear. But no. No forest lake turns up, no stag, not so much as a runaway spotted cow. But when he suddenly brakes at the lake that isn't there, when he throws his bike into a thicket of silence and turns and catches her as she starts to fall, when they sink into the grass in a shared confusion of zippers, hooks, narrow jeans legs, not only her mouth, but her whole body becomes a bubble. And not just a little nondescript plop, no, an Icelandic geyser, whose smoldering explosivity she's just learned about in school. And now that's started she imagines it as heaven-storming. She *is* a geyser: that much is clear. What isn't clear is the shadow, the slow gray film, that comes down afterwards from the beech trees and settles like a damp, mild melancholy over her face. And now one of two things could happen. With closed mouth he could stroke the shadow of salt on her cheeks. Or he could open his eyes, shake his head, say what the hell are you crying about?

# Pilot Project

It's night now. Defenseless
night. He's in my bed, his beard
scratches
like fiberglass and stars
itself against my throat
where he breathes, breathes, so I love
my buttocks and fat deposits
and my skin kamikaze-
brave to the end dares
to describe time.

# Open the Darkness

Held tight in the hips'
lead mold
and in wave after wave
of darkness
a stone ring
around my neck

I'm pushed
out over the deep

and open the darkness
with my mouth
a folded violet
two leaves
a cleft fruit
releases
its pain
and my body opens
in every membrane and out
beyond all borders

trembling
between my thighs
a voice calls

which is not mine

# SALT

Foam-sprayed black and white waves
of cows come rushing
down over the hill.
Until they stop at a hedge.
Abruptly. Suddenly. With their hooves
deep in a puddle and consider the owned.
Us who shudder
at the sight of dirt and the thick blue tongues
that shine like death.
And at the thought of lost chances the wolves pace
through our eyes: Has someone faxed
called or e-mailed? Would we miss something
if we threw ourselves plop in a ditch
and only breathed the air?
The cows stand
and lick salt
and stare until they are called in
by the drifting sky.

# ROOM SERVICE

That in all my hectic
activity I am suddenly from outside
being contemplated

with wondering dreaming
gentle irony

is a particular service I have received

and I owe my wholly special
heartfelt deep condition
to the neighbor's cow no. 76

who has stuck her head up
all at once at my window

with grass and clover
dripping from her muzzle.

# BLUE

The sun shimmers
on the hands-up spruces
and the blue silo
where a man holds fast to an iron railing
on the way up to a platform.
You can see his hands.
You can see his feet and imagine
he feels compelled
to count the 83 smooth steps
and the 80,000 clucking beings in the stalls below.
That he counts and counts, but dreams
of casting himself from the top
and in the last second before hitting earth
being caught up. Borne
by the wind's whisper
in the blue spruce.

## THE POTATOES

Hospital. In sinking
yellow gardens. Water
stands still
under the trees.

In a white bed lies
my immortal father.

Behind our closed eyes
we are busily
laughing
throwing leaves into the air
to make gold rain.
When we run
our feet swish.

Come evening we rake
the litter together,
make a bonfire.

In the air above the flames
his face is peeled
vibrating, naked

his glance in mine
before it congeals.

The potatoes in the ashes
are for me.

# THE MOVE

Can everything burn, can everything give light

after you died, father
I found an old cigar butt
on the planing-bench in your workshop

matches and avalanche

## VERTICAL

I saw my father balancing
on a ridge-pole. Dead. And with his arms
full of boards, canvas, helium
and little blue tacks. And with his heart fluttering
outside of his jacket and the cigar in his jaw,
young and warm
and as devil-may-care as he always was,
he ran out against the wind. And his path,
you ask me. Straight.
Straight up.
          That
I saw clearly. He shines
like a space-walker.

# Guardian Angels

They jump on broomsticks
bicycles and trains

to straddle by night
with pain and punishment
the bodies of the ambitious
in their beds

Then they magic
the trees green again

give little children
licorice
and three wishes

# WINTER

The sparrows whisper
in the dark at the back door

Every morning
I sprinkle salt
at their tails

# RIGHT THERE IN THE SMOKE

Right there in the woodsmoke, in the frost mist
thick
against the windowpane
       There
I can stand mornings in the kitchen
and let spoons teacups knives
drop
out of my hands

and fall into lead white
       out of every
fixed meaning
       And there
       right there
in the veil the sparrows
       throw up like a glittering
wall before my eyes

in an accidental
absent glance, suddenly
       slipping off to the side
I glimpse the border
of what can be said

The glowing border
       every body is wild
to touch.

# TIGHT-ROPE DANCER

Without a wobble hold the black
sucking eyes in check down there on both sides

And smile, smile
the *grimace d'artiste*

pivot on a knifeblade.

If I fall from the thin
vibrating line, if I break my neck

the audience will scream. And turn away
scratch its back.

# LETTER TO MY FLIGHTY DAUGHTER

Don't listen to me
when I say
you should obey

ignore me
when I say
humanity is lost

don't look
when every day I show you
my programmed life

use my safety nets
but unveil them
when they become ingenious traps

use my helping hands
but break away
when they become ugly tentacles
that surround and deform you

don't look
don't listen to me
don't feel guilty

fly!

# Go Far

Go far
make a big detour
around silence

that quicksand is dangerous

forget
your ostrich longing

## It Begins Someplace

It begins someplace
in a coldness under
asphalted meadows

someplace in a stiffening
of yarrow stalks
birds and fish

their silvery bodies
begin a suddenly
aimless streaming

of white bellies
through air and water
begins as a ticking

silence
in every single
little glittering

spruce needle
tactful hands
begin

from behind
to place themselves over
our eyes and mouths

the poison
on its way
through the body

begins someplace

# WOUND

Cold comes from every corner.
It's snowing.
And from the train Europe looks like
a brittle romantic poem
in which the lakes close
their black moon-
lost eyes and trickling
roses can be lying in the ground
around a perfectly ordinary house
containing a perfectly ordinary family
and then suddenly seep out
like blood through
a snow-white bandage.

# MOURNING DOVES

My heart thumps
a door opens and slams
up and in
an introduction to torture
and what do you think
you know, a little boy grew up
a big boy left
the house, in winter
the dogs get ice between their toes and bite them bloody
*You goo-oo-ood God, you goo-oo-ood God*, you say, you
scraggly bird in a long endlessness
slapping your wings up in your tree
maybe you know where he
went? But like me
mourning doves are dumb as doorknobs
up and in
up and in
and traces everywhere

# CLOSE TO THE SHADOW

Never
so terrifyingly

close to
the shadow

stopped
in the body

a profile seen
through water

and sliding
chemical sleep

my doubtful arms
my own thighs

if they really exist

# WILD PURSUIT

To drown in wine
or water or chemical
blue intoxicants. There are many kinds of darkness
to go into just to lie there dead in rooms
named after animals. There are many kinds of dissolved
in sobbing tears forms of dog or hare
to chase out of the body. You only have to
bare your teeth, white wild cruel
shining like human.

# GRIEF HAS STAMPED

Grief has stamped
a rose
a strange courage
on my mouth
to express contrary opinions
anger
and furious
declarations of love
every impulse
in Bengal flarelight
for one blink of an eye
nothing hidden
when my mouth's petals
burst open
in the ragged vocables
pain-courage
has seared on my lips

# A STONE IN THE BELLY

A stone in the belly. Strike water
from stone and divide it
in your body. You have to practice.
Cooling your skin. Pressing your face
down in the dark
scented forest floor, slowly
to get used to moving
in and out of grief. You have to practice.

# LOSE YOURSELF IN ME

Lose yourself in me
your rhythm pulses
on your tongue
a whirled up
angst
despair
touch with your lips
the floor
of feeling
touch
the hot walls
of death distilled
to darkness
melted down
to fields of violets
blue seconds
one night I have the rhythm's
fleeting help
in a fragrance
drifting out
of the corners of my mouth

# THE SWALLOW

Now here comes a swallow
to set alight my eyes.
It hangs there a moment and resembles joy.
What else can joy find to whisper?
That everything can be understood
in many different ways as proclaimed by modern physics
is no real solace.
Only that someone will whisper, and you feel
a tickle at the bottom of your ear
so you start smiling
because who whispers lies
so sweetly.

# THE THIRTEENTH MONTH

January morning.
New fallen snow. Now my friends too
are beginning to die in a column
in the newspaper and snow so thick, the garden surrenders.
Surrenders its role as well-kept lawns, beds
with blushing summer-mild phlox. And in this light
there is no one who has any need to hop in the car
looking radiantly sunburned
and happy. No one exists forever.
And no one consists
of anything more than water and maybe some other
molecules of longing, the whole thing the eating
feeling of hunger. To grasp
the thirteenth month. Whose light
is a chance to fill your yard with living
shouting small children with sleds.
To throw yourself down on your back in the new fallen snow
and with outspread arms

# MAYBE TODAY

Maybe today the shutters fly away
And something comes in
It sits on my hand

Around midnight it demands wine

# THROUGH ME

A flock of goats purls
over a stony field

a deep joy flies through me
its wings are
an old despair

# WE DRAW NEAR

We summon courage.
We draw near.
To breathe in deeply someplace
where our indolent
imperfect bodies can open:
Here is my emptiness.
Show me yours. Perhaps it is
the old black and white gnarled tangle
of stiffness, stubbornness, perhaps
an old glacier we touch
and mark how the cheeks
taste salt we draw near
a place we melt

# THANK-YOU NOTE

I don't have a name for the address
I don't know if the letter is to God
to the brain's own chemical processes
or which angel in the world I should thank
that I with all my doubt and burns
one morning can be like a forgiven child
and play
on a sounding-board of oblivion

# A SHARED SECOND

As if in the dark
someone or another
has struck
a match
and suddenly turned
his eyes
open
and white
in all
their death

I'm suddenly
not afraid
I don't look down
for the shared
second that streams
over our cheeks

clear
illumined

## WHEN I'M EATEN BY ANTS

When I'm eaten by ants
you'll see my house
through my skeleton
My cellars and towers
Stairways up down up
to the hovering balcony
from which I threw my love a rose
to the wall where I fell
and stayed a long time on my knees, bashed
my forehead bloody
Night is black. But lay your head back
and when you have sunk
to the bottom of the black
the stars will spring forth
When I'm eaten by ants
you'll see heaven
through my skeleton

# WINTER TREE

It's winter now, and according to statistics I should be dead. Drip, drip, one day I'm standing in a thaw and listening to the childhood chattering of Siberian grackles under a light gray sky that drizzles into puddles. Another day it's cold so my skin gets stiff and old and burnt by ice. And, too, different kinds of groaning and creaking in the walls of my inner cells and channels confirm that I, like the others growing in farther rows, must prepare myself for a soon and perhaps sudden felling. No one makes his own decision. And no one can in an instant's illumination mark his own sinking on a clearly charted route. Anyway I live just as much as always in the purple ice-flowers I dream at night while the snow accumulates and drifts like quilts on the small shoots growing around me. Anyway I breathe just as much as always, a voice pushes out in a rush of oxygen coming close to being a tongue, another word a whole body, and if I could choose it would end with lying down black against white in an easy to move away pile. Plain, no unneeded weight, whistled through by the wind, simple as haiku.

# ABOUT THE AUTHOR

Danish author and translator Inge Pedersen, born in Brønderslev in 1936, has published four collections of poems, two volumes of short stories, and two novels. The winner of many Danish and Scandinavian fellowships and prizes, she has received critical praise for the power and seriousness of her work, its imagery, its musical language, and its invitation to a richer experience of reality. She taught German for many years at the Nørre Nissum College of Education in Jutland, and lives in Jutland with her husband, Bent, who is also a writer.

# ABOUT THE TRANSLATOR

American poet and translator Marilyn Nelson, born in Cleveland in 1946, has published eight collections of poems, most recently *Fortune's Bones* (Front Street), *A Wreath for Emmett Till* (Houghton Mifflin Children's Division), and *The Cachoeira Tales and Other Poems* (LSU Press). She has been Poet Laureate of Connecticut since 2000. In 2004 she founded Soul Mountain Retreat, a small writers' colony.